THE BOOK OF
BEGINNING
CIRCLE GAMES

Let's Make a Circle

REVISED EDITION

Also by John M. Feierabend, published by GIA Publications, Inc.:
The Book of Echo Songs
The Book of Call and Response
The Book of Fingerplays and Action Songs
The Book of Children's SongTales
The Book of Songs and Rhymes with Beat Motions
The Book of Pitch Exploration
The Book of Movement Exploration (*with Jane Kahan*)

For infants and toddlers:
The Book of Lullabies
The Book of Wiggles and Tickles
The Book of Simple Songs and Circles
The Book of Bounces
The Book of Tapping and Clapping

On compact disc for infants and toddlers:
'Round and 'Round the Garden: Music in My First Year!
Ride Away on Your Horses: Music, Now I'm One!
Frog in the Meadow: Music, Now I'm Two!

On DVD and Compact Disc by Peggy Lyman and John M. Feierabend:
Move It! Expressive Movements with Classical Music
Move It 2! Expressive Movements with Classical Music

G-5878

THE BOOK OF

BEGINNING CIRCLE GAMES

Let's Make a Circle

REVISED EDITION

Compiled by John M. Feierabend

GIA PUBLICATIONS, INC. · CHICAGO

G-5878
The Book of Beginning Circle Games (Revised Edition)
Compiled by John M. Feierabend
www.giamusic.com/feierabend

"Dona Maricota" (p. 20), "Leak Kanseng" (p. 34), and "Uga, Uga, Uga" (p. 17) come from the collection *Roots and Branches* by Patricia Shehan Campbell, Ellen McCullough-Brabson, and Judith Cook Tucker, © 1994, assigned 2009 to Plank Road Publishing, Inc. Used with permission.

Artwork: Tim Phelps
Editor: Lillie Feierabend
Layout: Nina Fox

Table of

Contents

Introduction

This book contains many wonderful games to play in circles. These Circle Games are one of the principal joys of childhood, especially when played outdoors! All of the Circle Games in this book have been passed down from generation to generation and are full of wonder, magic, and make-believe.

Some of these Circle Games are stationary games in which one child chases after another while the rest of the group does not move. Some of these games begin with stationary circles but end with traveling circles as, one by one, children join a group moving around the circle. And some of the Circle Games travel around and around, often ending with a surprise twist.

All of these Circle Games encourage a variety of developmentally appropriate behaviors. Social skills, cognitive development, creativity, language development, motor skills, and of course musical skills are all embedded in the play. The musical elements of melody, beat, structure, and expressiveness are also central to circle game songs. These games also provide an early opportunity for children to discover the vitality that can be created and shared by a community. It takes a community to cooperate and play these games. And that same community shares not only the rules but also the spirit and energy as they delight in the chase or glow at the ending surprise.

The elements that make these Circle Games enduring childhood favorites are the same elements that have made folk dances endure for many generations. In these precursors to folk dances, children discover the united spirit that song and movement can provide.

Enjoy!

John M. Feierabend

STATIONARY CIRCLES

Bow, Wow, Wow

Bow, wow, wow, Whose dog art thou?

Lit - tle Tom - my Tuck - er's dog. Bow, wow, wow.

Motions

Children stand in a circle. Every other child turns and faces his or her partner.

Bow, wow, wow
  Stamp three times.
Whose dog art thou?
  Shake a finger at each other three times.
Little Tommy Tucker's dog
  Turn in a half circle while holding partner's hands and arrive in partner's place.
Bow, wow, wow
  Jump three times while turning halfway around. End facing a new partner.

Hickety, Pickety

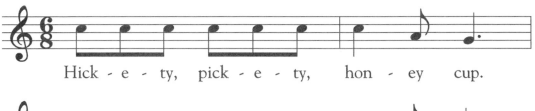

Hick - e - ty, pick - e - ty, hon - ey cup.

How man - y fin - gers do I hold up?

Motions

The children stand in a circle, facing center. One child stands behind another child and holds up 1, 2, 3, 4, or 5 fingers. After the class sings the song, the second child guesses how many fingers are held up.

The first child responds if incorrect.
"Three you said, but there were two."
Or if correct,
"Two you said, and there were two."

If the guess is correct, the two children trade places and the second child is the next to hold up fingers behind the next child in the circle. If the guess is wrong, the first child moves on to the next child in the circle.

The object of the game is to see who can remain the leader for the most turns.

I Have a Tree

I have a tree in my right hand, I have a

tree in my right hand, it bears ro -

ses in the month of May, It bears ro -

ses in the month of May. Get up, get

up, my fav - 'rite one, Get up, get

up, my fav - 'rite one, And pick the

one you like the best, And pick the one you like the best.

Children sit in a circle. During the first half of the song, one child walks around the outside of the circle. During the second half, the first child stops behind another and taps the beat on that child's shoulders. The two children change places. The game repeats with the new person walking around the circle.

In and Out the Window

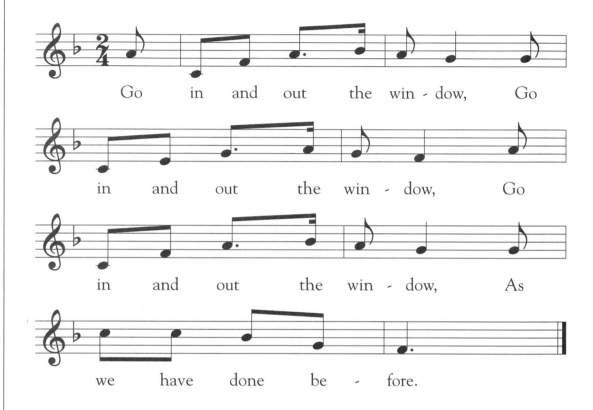

Go in and out the win-dow, Go
in and out the win-dow, Go
in and out the win-dow, As
we have done be-fore.

Verse 2

Go forth and choose your partner....

Verse 3

Go underneath the arches....

The children stand in a circle holding hands and raise hands to form arches. One child weaves in and out of the arches. During the second and third verses, that child chooses another and the two of them weave in and out of the arches. At the end of the third verse, the original child joins the circle and the game begins again with the new child weaving in and out of the arches.

Little Sally Walker

Lit - tle Sal - ly Walk - er, sit - ting in a sau - cer,

Rise, Sal - ly, rise, Wipe a - way your eyes.

Turn to the east and turn to the west and

turn to the one that you like the best.

Motions

Children stand in a circle while one child
sits in the center.

Motions for the child in the center:

Rise, Sally, rise
  Stand up.
Wipe your eyes
  Pretend to wipe eyes.
Turn to the east...
  Spin around with eyes covered and point.

At the end of the song, whomever is being
pointed to is the the next "Sally."

Muffin Man

Oh, do you know the muf - fin man, the

muf - fin man, the muf - fin man? Oh, do you know the

muf - fin man who lives on Dru - ry Lane?

Verse 1 (motions)

The children stand in a circle while one child walks or skips around the outside of the circle. At the end of the first verse, that child chooses another child.

Verse 2

Oh, yes I know the muffin man,
The muffin man, the muffin man.
Oh, yes I know the muffin man,
Who lives on Drury Lane.

The two children skip around the outside of the circle. At the end of the second verse, the original child returns to the circle. The game repeats with the new child going around the circle.

'Round and 'Round the Village

Go 'round and 'round the vil - lage, Go

'round and 'round the vil - lage, Go

'round and 'round the vil - lage, As

we have done be - fore.

Verse 1 (motions)

Children stand in a circle holding hands. Four other children walk or skip around the outside of the circle.

Verse 2

Go in and out the window...
As we have done before.

Children standing in the circle raise their hands, forming arches. Outside children weave in and out of the arches.

Verse 3

Now stand and face your partner...
And bow before you go.

Outside children stop and select partners by standing in front of a child and giving a bow or curtsey.

Verse 4

Now follow me to London...
As we have done before.

The four partners go to the outside of the circle and walk or skip around. At the end of the song the original four join the circle and the game repeats with the four new children walking around the outside of the circle.

Shooliloo

Leader: Just—— from the kitch - en, Group: Shoo - li - loo,

With a hand - ful of bis - cuits, Shoo - li - loo.

Oh—— Miss Mar - y, Shoo - li - loo,

Fly a - way o - ver yon - der, Shoo - li - loo.

Motions

Children sit in a circle on the floor, leaving a gap in the circle. The leader substitutes the name of a child for "Mary." When a child hears his or her name sung, that child gets up and "flies" to the gap left in the circle.

Uga, Uga, Uga! (Cake, Cake, Cake!) *Israeli*

U-ga, u-ga, u-ga   Ba-ma-a-gal na-chu-ga

Nis-to-ve-va kol-ha-yom   Ad ash-er nim-tza ma-kom La-

she-vet la-kum La-she-vet la-kum La-she-vet v' la-kum.

Motions

Students stand in a circle and join hands while they sing the song. During the third line, students sit on each repetition of the word "lashevet" and stand on "lakum."

General Translation

Cake, cake, cake.
We'll form a circle.
We'll go around all day long
Until we find a place to sit and
   stand.

Translation and Motions from *Roots and Branches* © 2009 Plank Road Publishing, Inc. Used with permission. Words by Ashman Aharon.

Uncle Jessie *Georgia Sea Islands*

1. Now, here comes Un - cle Jes - sie,
2. Now, here comes Un - cle Jes - sie, He's

Com-ing through the field,   With his horse and
look-ing ve - ry sad. He's lost his cot - ton

bug - gy and I know just how— he
and his corn and eve - ry - thing he

Clap: x x x x x

feels. Walk, walk,— Un - cle Jes - sie, walk, walk, walk,
had.

 x x x x   x x

— Un - cle Jes - sie, walk, walk, Step,— Un - cle Jes - sie,

 x x   x x

step, step, step,— Un - cle Jes - sie, step.

Verse 3

Now, if you want a sweetheart,
I'll tell you what to do,
Just take some salt and pepper
And sprinkle it in your shoe.

Verse 4

Now, if you want Uncle Jessie
To do what you want him to do,
You take some garlic and onion
And you put it in his shoe.

Motions

The group stands in a circle. During the verse, one child walks around the inside of the circle acting out the lyrics about Uncle Jessie. On the last note of the verse, the center child chooses someone from the circle to be their partner. The pair holds hands in the center of the circle during the chorus and dances the following two-step pattern: R-L-R-rest, L-R-L-rest, R-L-R-rest, L-R-L-rest. At the end of the chorus, the original center child returns to the circle, and their partner becomes the new center child. The dance repeats with the new center child and continues in the same pattern for the following verses and choruses.

Dona Maricota *Brazilian*

Do - na Ma - ri - co - ta, co - mo tem pas - sa - do? Por
Doh - na Mah-ree-coh - tah, coh - moh tay(m) pah - sah - doh? Pohr

on-de eu te-nho an-da-do tenho pas - sa - do mui - to bem. Me-
ohn - joo tay - noon dah-doh tay(n)oo pah - sah-doh mooee-too bay(m). Mee-

lhor eu pas - sa - ri - a se vo - cê fos - se meu bem.
loo reeoo pah - sah - ree - ah see voo - say foh - see meeoo bay(m).

Motions

Students sit or stand in a circle with one child in the center. As the students sing, the child in the center steps to the beat around the inside of the circle, pointing to each child he or she passes. On the very last word, "bem," the child in the center freezes and points to the nearest child, and the two children switch places.

General Translation

Dona Maricota,
How are you doing?
The places I have been,
I have had a good time.
But I would have a better time if
you were with me.

Hidden Objects

Black Snake

Black snake, black snake, where are you hid - ing?

Black snake, black snake, where are you hid - ing?

Motions

An object is hidden while one child is out of the room. When that child returns, he or she tries to find the "black snake." Meanwhile, the group sings the song repeatedly, singing softer when the child moves farther from the object and singing louder when the child moves closer to the object.

Biddy, Biddy

Jamaican

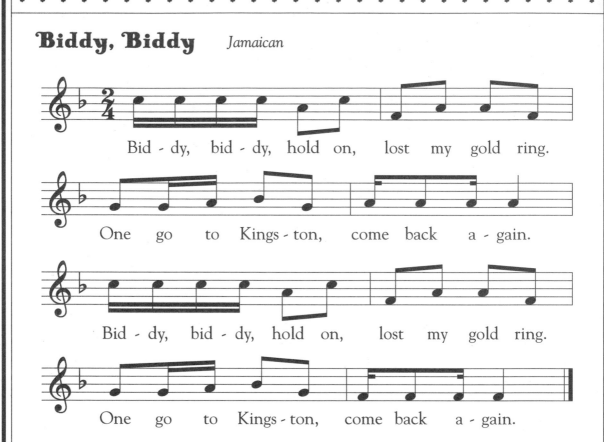

Bid - dy, bid - dy, hold on, lost my gold ring.

One go to Kings - ton, come back a - gain.

Bid - dy, bid - dy, hold on, lost my gold ring.

One go to Kings - ton, come back a - gain.

Motions

Children sit in a circle with hands behind their backs (or in front). One child sits in the center. The circle passes (or pretends to pass) a ring or coin. At the end of the song, the child in the center gets three guesses to discover who is really holding the ring. If the child guesses correctly, they get another turn; if not, the child holding the ring takes the place in the center.

Button You Must Wander

But - ton you must wan - der, wan - der, wan - der.

But - ton, you must wan - der ev - 'ry - where.

Bright eyes will find you. Sharp eyes will find you.

But - ton, you must wan - der ev - 'ry - where.

Motions

Children sit in a circle with hands behind their backs (or in front). One child sits in the center. A button is passed around the circle while the rest of the children pretend to be passing the button. At the end of the song, the child in the center gets three guesses to discover who is really holding the button. If the child guesses correctly, they get another turn; if not, the child holding the button takes the place in the center.

Bob-a-Needle

Oh, bob - a - nee - dle, bob - a - nee - dle, bob - a - nee - dle; where you

go - ing? Bob - a - nee - dle, bob - a - nee - dle, bob - a - nee - dle; can't

hide, bob - a - nee - dle, bob - a - nee - dle is a run - ning; bet - ter

hur - ry bob - a - nee - dle, bob - a - nee - dle is a run - ning; gon - na

catch you bob - a - nee - dle, bob - a - nee - dle is a run - ning;

Bob - a - nee - dle, bob - a - nee - dle is a run - ning;

Bob - a - nee - dle, bob - a - nee - dle's NOT a - run - ning.

You got bob - a - nee - dle!

Motions

Children sit in a circle and pass (or pretend to pass) an object with hands behind their back. One child sits in the middle of the circle and at the end of the song exclaims, "You got bob-a-needle!" and points to who they think has the object. If the child in the center guesses correctly, they get another turn. If the guess is not correct, the child holding the object comes to the center.

El Florón (The Flower) *Southwestern United States*

El flor - ón es - tá en las ma - nos y en las

ma - nos se ha de hal - lar. A - di - vi - nen quien lo

tie - ne o se que - da de plan - tón.

Motions

The group sits in a circle. One child sits in the middle with their eyes closed. A flower is passed around the circle while the song is sung. At the end of the song, the group places their hands behind their backs. The child in the center gets three chances to guess who is holding the flower.

General Translation

The big flower is in the hands and in the hands it is going to be found. Guess who has it or you will be standing up.

Chase Games in a Circle

A Tisket, a Tasket

A tis-ket, a tas-ket, a green and yel-low bas-ket, I

wrote a let-ter to my love and on the way I dropped it. I

dropped it, I dropped it, yes, on the way I dropped it. A

lit-tle (girl) picked it up and put it in (her) pock - et.
(boy)   (his)

Motions

The group sits in a circle. One child walks around the outside of the circle with a "letter." At the end of the second phrase, that child drops the "letter" behind some other child who picks up the letter and chases the first child around the circle.

The first child tries to reach the gap in the circle before being caught. The second child carries the letter around as the game is repeated.

Charlie Over the Ocean

Leader:

Group:

Char - lie o - ver the   o - cean,   Char - lie o - ver the   o - cean,

Char - lie o - ver the sea,   Char - lie o - ver the sea.

Char - lie caught a   big fish,   Char - lie caught a   big   fish,

Can't   catch   me,   Can't   catch   me.

Motions

One child walks around the outside of the circle of children and sings the leader part. At the end of the song, the leader taps another child on the shoulder and then runs around the circle trying to get to the gap in the circle before the other child can catch them.

Chase the Squirrel

Let us chase the squir - rel,

Up the hick - 'ry, down the hick - 'ry.

Let us chase the squir - rel

up the hick - 'ry tree.

Motions

Children stand in a circle holding hands with arms raised to make arches. One child (the hunter) and another child (the squirrel) start on opposite sides outside the circle. As the song is sung, the hunter must try to catch the squirrel. If the hunter catches the squirrel, she or he remains the hunter for another turn and the squirrel picks a new squirrel. If the squirrel evades the hunter, the squirrel may remain for another turn and the hunter picks a new hunter.

Cut the Cake

Clap your hands to-geth-er, Give a lit-tle shake.

Make a hap-py cir-cle, Then you cut the cake.

Motions

Children stand in a circle while one child walks around the outside of the circle. The children in the circle clap their hands, then shake their bodies, and then hold hands as they sing the song. When "cut the cake" is sung, the child walking around the outside stops and "cuts" through where two children are holding hands with the side of his or her hand. Those two children run in opposite directions around the outside of the circle. The original child stands in the gap and holds up one arm. The first of the two children back around the circle to touch the original child's outstretched hand becomes the next child to walk around the circle.

Grizzly Bear

Griz - zly bear, a griz - zly bear is sleep - ing in a cave. Please be ver - y qui - et, ver - y ver - y qui - et. If you wake him, if you shake him, he gets ver - y MAD!

Motions

Children stand in a circle, linking hands up high. One child (the bear) sits in the middle of the circle (the cave). Another child (the hunter) stands outside of the circle. At the end of the song the bear runs out of the circle. The children in the circle lower their arms except the two where the bear ran out leaving the entrance open to the cave. The bear must run around the circle one time and re-enter the cave without being caught by the hunter. If the hunter catches the bear, they remain the hunter; if not, they choose a new hunter. If the bear makes it back to the cave, they remain the bear; if not, they pick a new bear and the game is repeated.

Le Furet (The Ferret) *French*

Il court il court le fu - ret, Le fu - et du bois mes -

dames, Il court il court le fu - ret, Le fu - ret du bois jo -

li. Il est pas - sé par - i - ci, Il re - pas - se - ra par là.

Motions

Children sit on the floor in a circle. One child walks around the circle holding a stuffed animal (the ferret). At the end of the song, the first child drops the ferret behind another child, who picks up the ferret and chases the first child. The first child runs around the circle and tries to get back to the gap in the circle without getting caught.

General Translation

The ferret runs and runs in the woods, my ladies,
He runs and runs, the ferret in the beautiful woods.
He runs through here and runs back through there.

Little Swallow

Lit - tle Swal - low, fly to your nest,

Who goes there, fly a fly a - way now.

Lit - tle swal - low, fly to your nest,

fly a fly a - way.

Motions

Children sit in a circle. One child walks around the outside of the circle with a handkerchief. At the end of the song, he or she drops the handkerchief behind someone who picks it up and chases the first child around the circle. The first child tries to get back to the gap before being tagged.

Leak Kanseng (Hide the Scarf) *Cambodia*

Leak kan-seng chhma khaim keng oh long oh long.

Motions

Children sit on the floor in a circle. One child walks around the outside of the circle holding a scarf. While the children in the circle sing, the child holding the scarf drops it secretly behind another child. This child must be alert to realize the scarf holder no longer has the scarf. He or she picks up the scarf and chases the first child. The first child runs around the circle and tries to get back to the gap in the circle without getting caught.

General Translation

Hide the scarf!
The cat is biting his/her heel
And drags the leg.

Translation and Motions from *Roots and Branches* © 2009 Plank Road Publishing, Inc. Used with permission.

STATIONARY BECOMES TRAVELING

All Around the Buttercup

All a-round the but-ter-cup, one two, three.

If you want a pret-ty one, just choose me.

Motions

Children stand in a circle, linking hands to form arches. One child weaves in and out of the arches. At the end of the verse, the first child chooses one they are near, and the second child walks in front, leading the first child in and out of the arches. On each subsequent verse, the newest child walks in front leading the group in and out of the arches until there is only one child left.

Boom Makaleli

Group:
'Round and 'round we must go,

Group:
Boom ma - ka - le - li chee, chim, boom.

Group:
'Round and 'round we must go,

Group:
Boom ma - ka - le - li chee, chim, boom.

Solo:
Down Miss _____ you must go,

Group:
Boom ma - ka - le - li chee, chim, boom.

Motions

Children walk around in a circle while one child (the "leader") walks around the inside of the circle in the opposite direction. The leader sings "Down Miss ___" or "Down Mister ___" as the leader names another child and taps that child's shoulder. The second child and subsequent children must follow the "leader" around the inside of the circle in a crouch. Repeat until everybody is walking in a crouch.

Brown Bread and Butter

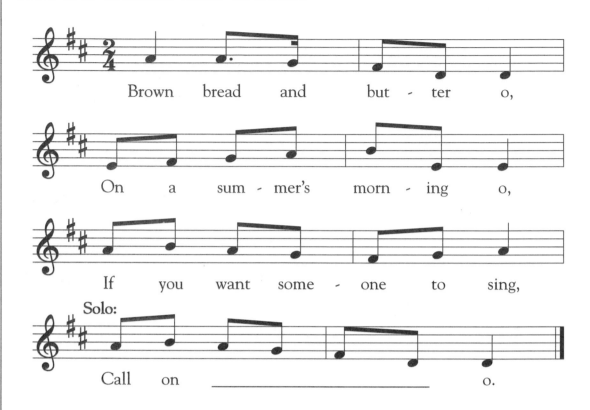

Brown bread and but - ter o,

On a sum - mer's morn - ing o,

If you want some - one to sing,

Solo:

Call on _____ o.

Verse 2

[Group] (M) is for (Mary) o,
[Group] On a summer's morning o,
[Group] If you want someone to sing,
[Solo]   Call on (Jumping Jason) o.

Motions

The group stands in a circle. One child walks around the inside of the circle. This child sings the last line of the verse solo, choosing the person that will join them. In naming the new person, the singer adds an adjective that begins with the same letter as the first letter of the chosen child's name, for example, Marching Mary or Pretty Pat. The whole group sings the first line of the second verse, using the new person's adjective and name. The newest person inside the circle sings the last line solo as she or he chooses another child. The game continues until there is only one child left and the whole class walks around that child. This last child will be the first when the game begins again.

The Farmer in the Dell

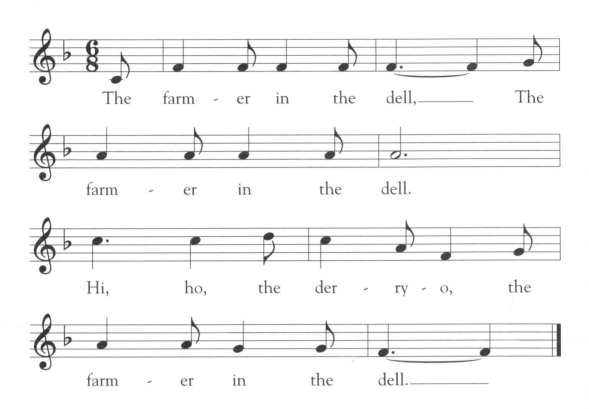

The farm - er in the dell,——— The

farm - er in the dell.

Hi, ho, the der - ry - o, the

farm - er in the dell.———

Additional Verses

2. The farmer takes a wife...
3. The wife takes a child...
4. The child takes a nurse...
5. The nurse takes a dog...
6. The dog takes a cat...
7. The cat takes a rat...
8. The rat takes the cheese...
9. The cheese stands alone...

Motions

The group stands in a circle while one child ("the farmer") walks around inside the circle during the first verse.

During the second verse, the "farmer" picks a "wife." The two walk around the inside of the circle holding hands. During verses two through eight, the newest person inside the circle chooses another child to join the group holding hands and walking inside the circle. During verse nine, everybody except the "cheese" rejoins the circle. The "cheese" stands in the middle of the circle as the group claps hands while singing. The "cheese" becomes the "farmer," and the game repeats from the beginning.

Go In and Out the Window

Go in and out the win-dow, Go
in and out the win-dow, Go in and out the
win-dow, As we have done be-fore.

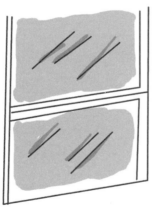

Motions

The group stands in a circle and extends hands up to form arches. One child weaves in and out of the arches. At the end of the song, that child picks another child, and the two of them weave in and out of the arches. The newest child selected chooses the next child to join the line. Continue until there is only one child left. That child will be the first child to weave the next time the game is played.

Here Comes a Bluebird

Here comes a blue-bird through my win-dow.

Here comes a blue-bird through my win-dow.

Here comes a blue-bird through my win-dow.

Hi - did-dle dum dee.

Motions

The group stands in a circle and extends hands up to form arches. One child weaves in and out of the arches. At the end of the song, that child picks another child, and the two of them weave in and out of the arches. The newest child selected chooses the next child to join the line. Continue until there is only one child left. That child will be the first child to weave the next time the game is played.

Little Bird

Lit-tle bird, lit-tle bird, fly through my win-dow.

Lit-tle bird, lit-tle bird, fly through my win-dow.

Lit-tle bird, lit-tle bird, fly through my win-dow and

buy mo-las-ses can-dy. Go through my win-dow,

my sug-ar lump, Go through my win-dow, my sug-ar

lump, And buy mo-las-ses can-dy.

Motions

The group stands in a circle and extends hands up to form arches. One child weaves in and out of the arches. At the end of the song, that child picks another child, and the two of them weave in and out of the arches. The newest child selected chooses the next child to join the line. Continue until there is only one child left. That child will be the first child to weave the next time the game is played.

My Little Boat

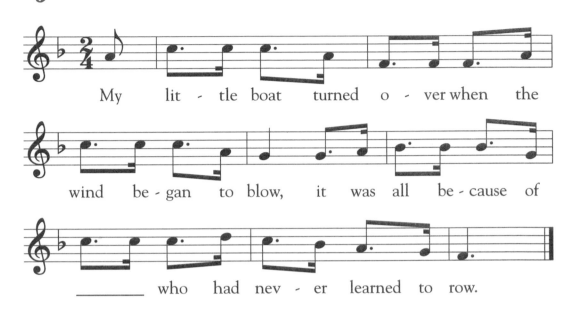

My lit - tle boat turned o - ver when the

wind be - gan to blow, it was all be - cause of

_____ who had nev - er learned to row.

Verse 2

If I were a fishy
And could swim down in the sea,
I'd rescue little _____
And I'd take him (her) home with me.

Motions

Children stand in a circle. One child walks around the circle and chooses another child by tapping his or her shoulder and inserting that child's name into the song. The pair hold hands and walk around the circle.

The second child and each subsequent child choose another child as described above. All of the children hold hands while walking in a line around the circle.

The game continues until all children have been "rescued."

Old Bald Eagle

Old bald ea - gle sails a - round,

Day - light is gone,

Old bald ea - gle sails a - round,

Day - light is gone.

Motions

The group stands in a circle while one child walks around the inside of the circle. At the end of the song, the child in the center chooses another child to join him or her. The class now sings "Two bald eagles sail around…" Continue until all children are walking around in a circle.

Old King Glory

Old King Glo-ry on the moun-tain,— The

moun-tain was so high,— it near-ly touched the sky. The

first one, the sec-ond one, the third one fol-low me.

Motions

The group stands in a circle while one child walks around the outside of the circle. That child taps on the shoulders of three children when "the first one, the second one, the third one" is sung. Only the third child follows the child(ren) outside the circle. The newest person outside the circle taps three other children on the shoulder. The song repeats until only one child remains. That child is "king of the mountain" and should be first the next time the game is played.

One Elephant

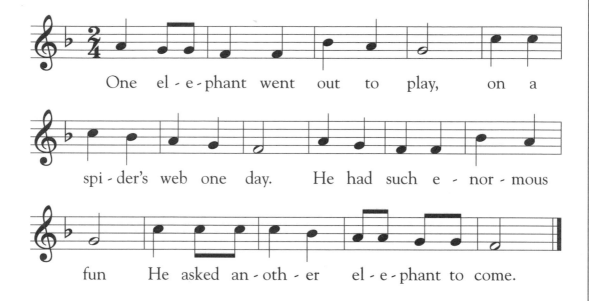

One el-e-phant went out to play, on a spi-der's web one day. He had such e-nor-mous fun He asked an-oth-er el-e-phant to come.

Motions

The group stands in a circle. One child walks around the inside of the circle while leaning over, clasping his or her hands to make an elephant's trunk and swinging the "trunk" from side to side. At the end of the song, they choose another child who follows behind while the group sings, "Two elephants went..." Continue until all of the children are walking around in a circle.

Variation

(Tails and Trunks; for older children)

The first child extends one hand between his or her legs and joins hands with the child behind. As each child joins the line, he or she extends one hand to the person in front and one hand behind and between his or her legs, to link with the person in back.

Un Elefante (One Elephant) *Mexican*

Un el - e - fan - te ba - lan - ce - a - ba

Sob - re la te - la de u - na a - ra - ña,

Co - mo ve - í - a que re - sis - tí - a,

lla - mó a o - tro el - e - fan - te.

Verse 2

Dos elefantes balanceaban sobre la tela de una arña,
Como veían que resistía, llamaron a otro elefante.

General Translation

One elephant balanced on a spider's web.
When he found out it would hold him, he asked another to join him.

Motions

The group stands in a circle. One child walks around the inside of the circle while leaning over, clasping his or her hands to make an elephant's trunk and swinging the "trunk" from side to side. At the end of the song, they choose another child who follows behind while the group sings, "Dos elefantes balanceaban…" Continue until all of the children are walking around in a circle.

Variation

(Tails and Trunks; for older children)

The first child extends one hand between his or her legs and joins hands with the child behind. As each child joins the line, he or she extends one hand to the person in front and one hand behind and between his or her legs, to link with the person in back.

Needle and Thread

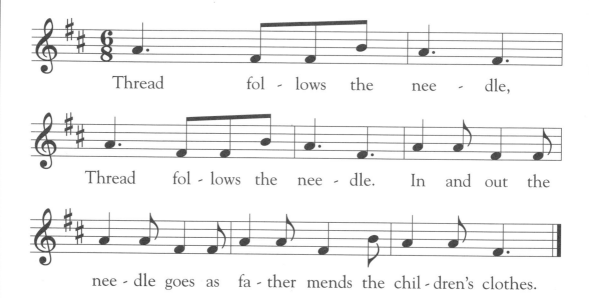

Thread fol - lows the nee - dle,

Thread fol - lows the nee - dle. In and out the

nee - dle goes as fa - ther mends the chil - dren's clothes.

Motions

The group stands in a circle with arms up. One child weaves in and out among the other children. At the end of the song, he or she chooses another child to join them. The game repeats until the entire group is traveling in a circle.

TRAVELING CIRCLES

Al Corro de la Patata *Spanish*

Al co - rro de la pa - ta - ta, co - me - re - mos en - sa -

la - da co - mo co - men los se - ño - res, na - ran -

Spoken:

ji - tas y li - mo - nes. ¡A chu - pé, a chu -

pé! Sen - ta - di - ta me que - dé.

Motions

The group walks around in a circle and falls down at the end.

General Translation

Ring around the potato
Eating salad greens with tomato
Like gentle people eat,
Eating citrus fruits so sweet.
To the ground
We all fall down!

Allee Galloo

Al-lee gal-loo, gal-loo.   Al-lee gal-loo, gal-lee.

Al - lee   gal - loo, gal-loo, gal-lee, WHEEE!

Motions

Walk around in a circle and kick foot up
high with the last word.

Built My Lady

Built my la-dy a fine brick house, Built it in a

gar-den. I put her in but she jumped out, so

fare thee well my— dar-lin'.

Motions

Children stand in a circle and make groups of three. Each group has two children holding hands and the third child standing between those two children. During the first two phrases, the two children holding hands walk around the third child in the center. During the third and fourth phrases the child in the middle ducks under and out of the two holding him or her and moves to the next couple, ducks under and into their "house." Repeat until children return to their original "house."

Down in the Valley

Down in the val - ley, two by two,— Oh, ba - by

two by two,— Oh, ba - by two by two. Down in the val - ley

two by two.— Now, rise, sug - ar, rise.

Verse 2

Let me see you make a motion two
by two...

Verse 3

Choose another partner, two by two...

Motions

During verse one, children walk around in a circle "two by two."

During verse two, children on inside circle make a motion during the first half of the verse. Their partner imitates the motion during the second half of the verse.

During verse three, each person goes to find a new partner and, holding their partner's hands, regroup in a circle "two by two."

Francisco

Take off your shoes and stock - ings, And

if your feet go bare, Fran -

- C - I - S - CO, C - I - S - CO,

Shake it if you care, Oh!

Verse 2

Oh, shake it, baby, shake it,
Shake it if you can,
Shake it like a milkshake,
And drink it like a man.

Verse 3

Oh, rumble to the bottom,
Rumble to the top,
You turn yourself around and 'round
And then you have to stop.

Motions

*During the first verse, children walk
around in a circle with one child in the
center walking in the opposite direction.
During the second verse, the child in the
center shakes in some manner and the
children in the circle imitate his or her
motion. During the third verse, everyone
shakes down to the ground and back up.
The one in the center covers his or her
eyes and turns around pointing. At the
end of the song, the child who is pointed to
becomes the next one in the center.*

Our Gallant Ship

Three times a-round went our gal-lant ship, And

three times a-round went she.

Three times a-round went our gal-lant ship and we

sank to the bot-tom of the sea.

Motions

Children walk around in a circle. Sink to the ground at the end of the song. Chant the following rhyme while tapping on the floor:

Penny on the water,
Penny on the sea,
Up jumps a little fish
And up jumps me!

Jump up and be ready to repeat the song.

OR sing the second verse as the children continue to hold hands while getting up.

Verse 2

"Pull her up, pull her up," said the
  little sailor boy,
"Pull her up, pull her up," said he,
"Pull her up, pull her up," said the
  little sailor boy,
"Or we'll sink to the bottom of the
  sea."

Gira, Gira Tondo *Italian*

Gi-ra, gi-ra ton-do, Il pa-ne sot-toil for-no, Un

maz-zo di vi-o-le, Le do-no a chi le vuo-le; Le

vuo-le la San-dri-na, E cas-chi la liù pic-ci-na.

General Translation

Ring around we go. Bread is baking.
Pick a bunch of violets and give
them to someone who wants them.
We'll give them to the tallest. And
the smallest one falls down.

Motions

*The group walks around in a circle and
"falls down" at the end of the song.*

See a variation of this song on page 70.

Ickle Ockle

Ick - le ock - le, blue bot - tle, fish - es in the sea.

If you want a part - ner, please choose me.

Motions

This game is played with an odd number of children. Children walk around in a circle with one child in the center. At the end of the song, the one in the middle grabs one child to be his or her partner. All the others run to the center and grab partners. The one left without a partner is the next one in the center and the game is repeated.

La Rueda de San Miguel *Mexican*

Rue - da, rue - da, San Mi - guel, San Mi - guel,

to - do traen su ca - ja de miel.

A lo ma - du - ro, a lo ma - du - ro,

que se vol - te - e _____ de bur - ro.

General Translation

The wheel of San Miguel,
  San Miguel;
Everybody brings his honey box.
Ready, ready,
Have (him) (her) turn, _____
  of donkey.

Motions

Children walk around in a circle holding hands. As each child's name is called that child turns facing out without letting go of his or her hands. That child will have one hand crossed in front and one hand crossed in back. When the song repeats she or he calls the next child's name. Continue until all children's names have been called. Start the game over again; this time as each child's name is called, they uncross their arms.

Las Estatuas de Marfil *Mexican*

A las es - ta - tuas de mar -

fil, u - no, dos, y tres a - sí.

Motions

Students walk in a circle while singing the song, and one student stands in the middle of the circle. At the end of the song, students freeze in statue poses. The student in the middle can pick the pose they like best and switch with that student.

From *El Patio de Mi Casa* (G-6947). Used with permission.

Little Red Caboose

Lit-tle red ca-boose, Lit-tle red ca-boose,

Lit-tle red ca-boose be-hind the train.— Toot, toot,

Smoke-stack on its back, Rol-lin' down the track,

Lit-tle red ca-boose be-hind the train.— Toot, toot.

Motions

Children follow a leader as he or she weaves around the room. At the end of the song, the leader becomes the caboose and the next in line becomes the new leader.

Looby Loo

Here we go loo - by loo. Here we go loo - by lie.

Here we go loo - by loo, All on a Sat - ur - day

night.___ You put your right hand in,___ You

put your right hand out.___ You give your-self a

shake, shake, shake, and turn your-self a - bout.

Additional Verses

2. You put your left hand in...
3. You put your right foot in...
4. You put your left foot in...
5. You put your whole self in...

Here We Go 'Round the Mulberry Bush

Here we go 'round the mul - ber - ry bush,

mul - ber - ry bush, mul - ber - ry bush.

Here we go 'round the mul - ber - ry bush, So

ear - ly in the morn - ing.

Additional Verses

2. This is the way we wash our clothes...
3. This is the way we wring out our clothes...
4. This is the way we hang up our clothes...
5. This is the way we iron our clothes...
6. This is the way we fold our clothes...

Motions

Walk around in a circle during the first verse. During the other verses pantomime the motions suggested. Have children make up other verses.

No Bears Out Tonight

No bears out to-night, No bears out to-night,

No bears out to-night, They've all gone a-way.

Motions

The group walks around in a circle and squats down at the end of the song.

Oats, Peas, Beans and Barley

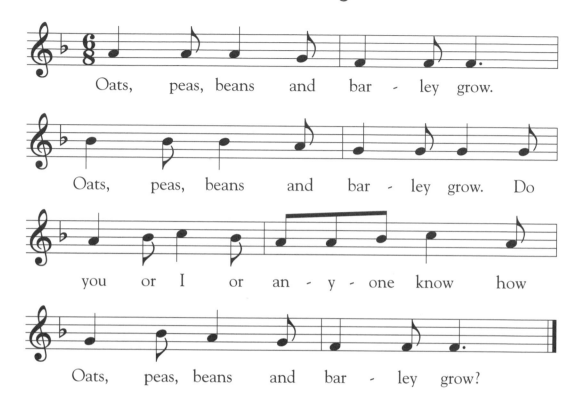

Oats, peas, beans and bar - ley grow.

Oats, peas, beans and bar - ley grow. Do

you or I or an - y - one know how

Oats, peas, beans and bar - ley grow?

Verse 1

Walk around in a circle while singing.

Verse 2

Stand still and pantomime motions as follows:

First the farmer plants the seeds
Swing arms gently as if tossing seeds into a field.

Then he stands and takes his ease.
Stand still with arms folded.
He stomps his foot
Stomp foot once with the word "stomps."
And claps his hands
Clap hands once with the word "claps."
And turns around to see the land.
With hand to forehead, turn around once.

Our Boots

Our boots are made of leath - er, Our stock - ings are made of silk, Our skirts are made of cal - i - co As white as an - y milk. Here we go a - round and a - round, Un - til we touch the ground. Here we go a - round and a - round, Un - til we touch the ground.

Motions

During the first half of the song, the group walks around in a circle in pairs. During the second half, each pair turns around in place while holding hands, slowly sinking to the ground.

Paw-Paw Patch

Where, oh where is dear lit-tle Nel-lie?

Where, oh where is dear lit-tle Nel-lie?

Where, oh where is dear lit-tle Nel-lie?

Way down yon-der in the paw-paw patch.

Additional Verses

2. Come on friends, let's go find her...
3. Pickin' up paw-paws, puttin' in your pocket...
4. Hold her tight so we don't lose her...

Motions

The group forms a circle holding hands while one child ("Nellie") goes somewhere in the room outside the circle. During verse one, the class walks around in a circle. During verse two, one child, selected to be the leader, leads the class in a line and encircles "Nellie." During verse three, all children reach down and pretend to pick up paw-paws (touch the floor) and put them in their pockets (tap on thighs). During verse four, the child who was at the end of the line holds hands with "Nellie," bringing "Nellie" into the line, and the leader takes the group back to the original place and forms a circle. Another "Nellie" is selected and the game begins again.

Savez-vous Planter des Choux? *French Canadian*

Chorus

Sa-vez-vous plant-er des choux? A la mod-e, A la mod-e.

Sa-vez-vous plant-er des choux? A la mod-e, de chez-nous.

Verses

1. On les plante avec nos doigts
   A la mode, A la mode
   On les plante avec nos doigts
   A la mode, de chez nous.
   (Chorus)

2. On les plante avec nos pieds...
   (Chorus)

3. On les plante avec nos coudes...
   (Chorus)

4. On les plante avec nos têtes...
   (Chorus)

General Translation

Chorus: Do you know how we plant cabbage? Watch and see.
Verse 1: We plant with our fingers.
Verse 2: We plant with our two feet.
Verse 3: We plant with our elbows.
Verse 4: We plant with our heads.

Motions

Chorus:
   All children walk around in a circle.
Verses 1–4:
   All children stand in a circle and make digging motions with the body parts mentioned.

Peep Squirrel

Group:

Peep squir - rel, peep squir - rel,

do - da, did - dle - um, do - da, did - dle - um,

Peep squir - rel, peep squir - rel,

Solo:

do - da, did - dle - um, dum. I've

got to get out of here, day's a - break - in',

sun's a - ris - ing, bet you five dol - lars I'll get out of here.

Motions

The circle walks around in one direction while one child (the hunter) walks in the opposite direction on the outside of the circle. Another child (the squirrel) stands in the center of the circle. After the squirrel sings the last two phrases of the song, the circle stops, holds hands, and raises their arms to form arches. The squirrel leaves the circle through one of the arches and tries to run around the circle and back inside through that same arch without being caught by the hunter. If the squirrel evades the hunter, he or she remains the squirrel for another turn and a new hunter is chosen. If the hunter catches the squirrel, the hunter remains for another turn and a new squirrel is chosen.

Ring a Ring a Roundo

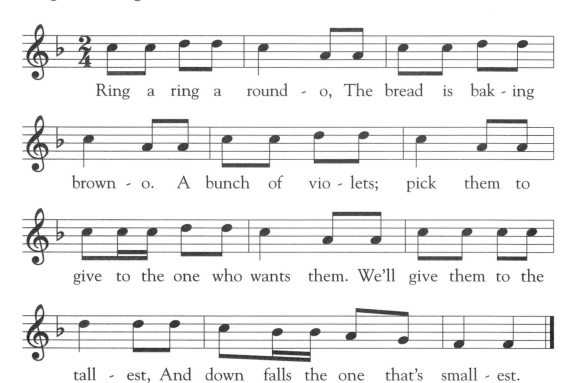

Ring a ring a round - o, The bread is bak - ing brown - o. A bunch of vio - lets; pick them to give to the one who wants them. We'll give them to the tall - est, And down falls the one that's small - est.

Motions

The group walks around in a circle and "falls down" at the end.

See a variation of this song on page 56.

Ring Around the Rosie

Ring a-round the ros-ie, A pock-et full of po-sies.

Ash-es, ash-es, we all fall down!

Motions

The group joins hands and walks around in a circle. Everyone "falls down" at the end of the verse. After falling down, tap hands on the floor and recite the following rhyme:

The cows are in the meadow
Eating buttercups.
A tish-oo, a tish-oo,
We all jump up!
 Jump up.

Verse 2
A bird upon the steeple,
Sits high above the people,
Ashes, ashes,
We all kneel down.
 Kneel down.

Verse 3
The king has sent his daughter,
To fetch a pail of water,
Ashes, ashes,
We all bow down.
 Bow.

Verse 4
The wedding bells are ringing,
The boys and girls are singing,
Ashes, ashes,
We all fall down.
 Fall down.

Ringo, Ringo, Rango

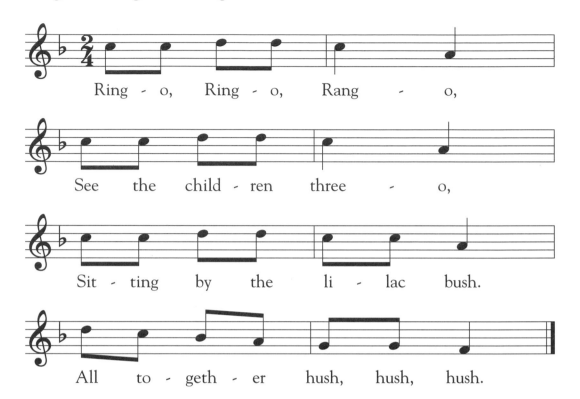

Ring - o, Ring - o, Rang - o,

See the child - ren three - o,

Sit - ting by the li - lac bush.

All to - geth - er hush, hush, hush.

Motions

Children walk around in a circle with one
child in the center. At the end of the song,
the children in the circle squat down and
shut their eyes. The child in the center
chooses another child and trades places.
The new child in the center chants,
"Come out, come out wherever you are."
The children in the circle open their eyes
and repeat the game.

Rosie, Darling Rosie

Leader: Ros - ie, dar - ling Ros - ie, Ha - ha Ros - ie,

Ros - ie dar - ling Ros - ie, Ha - ha Ros - ie,

Way down yon - der in Bal - ti - more, Ha - ha Ros - ie,

Need no car - pet on my floor, Ha - ha Ros - ie.

Group:

Verse 2

Grab your partner and follow me...
Let's go down by Gallee...
Rosie, darling, hurry...
If you don't mind you're gonna get
    left...

Verse 3

You steal my partner, you won't steal
    no more...
Better stay away from my back door...
Stop right still and study yourself...
See that fool where she got left...

Motions

*One circle forms inside another circle.
Those two circles walk around in the same
direction. During the first verse, one child
walks "through the alley" between the two
circles in the opposite direction that the
circles are moving. During the second
verse, the single child chooses one child
from either circle and the two of them walk
"through the alley." During the third
verse, the original child goes to the vacant
space, and the game repeats with the
chosen child walking "through the alley."*

Sally Go 'Round the Sun

Sal-ly go 'round the sun,   Sal-ly go 'round the moon,

Sal-ly go 'round the chim-ney pot,   Ev-'ry af-ter-noon. BOOM!

Motions

Children walk around in a circle. When they shout "BOOM," they jump up and turn halfway around so that they end up facing the opposite direction. Repeat the song while walking in the opposite direction.

Santa Maloney

Here we go Santa Ma - lo - ney.

Here we go San - ta Ma - lo - ney.

Here we go San - ta Ma - lo - ney, as

we go 'round a - bout.

Motions

Children walk around in a circle with the song. At the end of the song the circle stops and one child selects a motion that all children imitate following that child's tempo. Sing words appropriate to the action such as "Tap your hand on your knee." Then the group sings the original song again while walking around in a circle. Continue repeating the song until each child has had a turn to make up an action.

Shoo Turkey

Leader:
Lit - tle girl, lit - tle boy.   Group: Yes ma'am.

Well, did you go to town?   Yes ma'am.

Well did you get an - y eggs?   Yes ma'am.

Well did you bring them home?   Yes ma'am.

Well did you cook an - y bread?   Yes ma'am.

Well did you save me mine?   Yes ma'am.

All:
Then, shoo tur - key, shoo, shoo. Shoo tur - key, shoo, shoo.

Motions

Children stand in a circle during the call and response. During the last phrase, children walk around in a circle "shooing" the turkey with both hands, first to one side and then to the other.

Snail, Snail

Snail,   snail,   snail,   snail,

go   a - round   and   'round   and   'round.

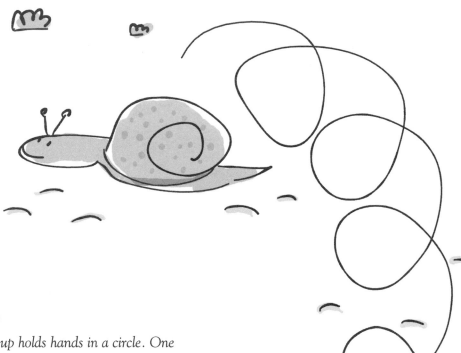

Motions

The group holds hands in a circle. One child (the leader) breaks the circle and leads the group on an inward spiral. When the leader reaches the center, she or he takes the line on an outward spiral traveling between the rows of children still on the inward spiral. When finished, the circle will be facing out. Perform another inward and outward spiral to bring the children back to facing toward the center.

Take Your Feet Out the Sand

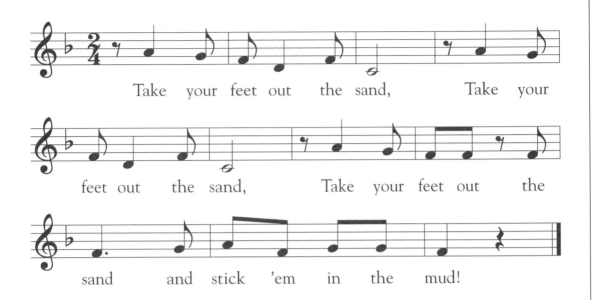

Take your feet out the sand, Take your

feet out the sand, Take your feet out the

sand and stick 'em in the mud!

Motions

The group travels around the room as if lifting feet out of sand.

Create additional verses and motions by changing the word "sand."

Examples:
Take your feet out the snow...
Take your feet out the jello...
Take your feet out the cement...

The Leaves Are Green

The leaves are green, the nuts are brown. They
hang so high they won't come down.
Leave them a - lone 'til frost - y weath - er and
they will all___ fall down to - geth - er.

Motions

*The group walks around in a circle and
"falls down" at the end.*

This Lady She Wears

This la‑dy she wears a dark green shawl, A

dark green shawl, a dark green shawl, This la‑dy she wears a

dark green shawl, I love her to my heart.

Verse 1 (motions)

The children stand in a circle with one child in the center of the circle. Before the song begins, the child in the center chooses three words to describe something they are wearing. During the first verse, the children walk in a circle. The child in the middle walks in the opposite direction.

Verse 2

Now choose you a partner,
  honey my love,
Honey my love, honey my love,
Now choose you a partner,
  honey my love,
I love you to my heart.
  The child in the center chooses another and continues walking with that new partner in the opposite direction.

Verse 3

Farewell to your partner,
  honey my love....
  The original child joins the circle and the second child continues walking in the opposite direction. At the end of the verse, the child in the center chooses three words to describe something they are wearing. The game continues.

Walk Along John

Group:

Come on boys and hush your talk - ing,

All join hands and let's go walk - ing,

Solo:

Walk a - long John, with your (pa-per col-lar) on,

Group:

Walk a - long John, with your (pa-per col-lar) on.

Motions

The children stand in a circle and sing the song while one child walks around the inside of the circle. The third phrase is sung by the child in the center as she or he takes another child by the hand, incorporating the new child's name, some article and color of clothing into the song. ("Walk along Jason, with your blue shirt on.") The group repeats the third phrase. The game continues with the last person in the group choosing a new person and singing the third phrase by him or herself. Repeat the game until all children have been chosen.

Walk, Daniel

Walk, Dan-iel, walk, Dan-iel. Walk, Dan-iel,

walk, Dan-iel. The oth-er way, Dan-iel.

The oth-er way, Dan-iel.

Motions

During the first phrase, children walk around in a circle. During the second phrase, children turn around and return where they started.

Additional Verses

2. Rock, Daniel...
3. Give me the knee bone bend, Daniel...
4. Fly, Daniel...
5. *(create new motions)*

Wind the Bobbin

Wind the bob - bin, ding dong. Gon - na

wind it tight, ding dong.

Bob - bin a - wound up, bob - bin a - wound up,

Bob - bin a - wound up, ding dong. Gon - na
(Break it!)

Motions

The children hold hands. One child is the anchor and does not move his or her feet. The leader takes the line around and around the anchor until the line is "wound up." When "wound up" as far as possible, shout "Break it!" and all children let go of their hands.

Pass Under the Arch

Que Pase el Rey (The King May Pass) *Colombian*

Que pase el Rey, Que ha de pa - sar, Que el
hi - jo del Con - de se ha de que - dar.

Motions

Two children hold hands and lift them to form an arch. One child will be the "sun" and the other will be the "moon." The rest of the children form a circle and pass under the arch. At the end of the song, the arch drops and "captures" one of the children. The "captured" child whispers "sun" or "moon" into the ear of one of the children forming the arch and stands behind the corresponding child. When all the children have been captured and are standing in one of the lines, everyone grabs the waist of the person in front, and a tug of war ensues.

Translation

The King may pass,
The King will pass,
But the son of the Count
Will have to stay.

La Fuente (The Fountain) *Cuban*

Group:
Al á - ni - mo, al á - ni - mo, la fuen - te se rom -

Arch:
pió. Al á - ni - mo, al á - ni - mo, mem -

Group:
dad - la á com - po - ner. Al á - ni - mo, al á - ni - mo, ¿de

Arch:
que se ha - ce el di - ne - ro? *Al á - ni - mo, al*

Group:
á - ni - mo, de cas - ca - ra - de hue - vo. U - ri, u - ri, u -

rai, la rei - na va á pa - sar. Los del an - te cor - ren

mu - cho y el de a - trás se que - da - rá.

General Translation

Skip lively now. The fountain has
been broken.
Skip lively now. We'll have to
mend it.

Skip lively now. What will we use
for money?
Skip lively now. We'll have to use
an eggshell.

Oh me, oh my,
The queen will come today.
The ones in front may pass by,
But the last one has to stay.

Motions

*Two children hold hands and lift them to
form an arch. One child will be "roses"
and the other will be "jasmine." The rest
of the children form a circle and pass
under the arch. At the end of the song, the
arch drops and "captures" one of the
children. The "captured" child whispers
"roses" or "jasmine" into the ear of one
of the children forming the arch and is told
which person to stand behind. After the
last child has chosen "roses" or "jasmine,"
everybody grabs the waist of the person in
front, and a tug of war ensues.*

Como la Víbora (Like the Snake) *Mexican*

A la ví - bo - ra, ví - bo - ra de la mar,

de la mar, por a - quí pue - den pa - sar;

Los de a de - lan - te co - rren mu - cho, y los de a - trás se

que - da - rán, ¡tras, tras, tras!

Motions

Two children hold hands and make an arch for the other children to pass under. As the last word is sung, the arch drops, trapping one person. That person trades places with one of the two people who are making the arch.

General Translation

Like the snake swimming in the sea.
Through this bridge pass quickly;
Those in front go through fast,
Those in the back are last, last, last.

London Bridge

Lon - don Bridge is fall - ing down,

fall - ing down, fall - ing down.

Lon - don Bridge is fall - ing down,

My fair la - dy.

Additional Verses

2. London Bridge is half built up...
3. London Bridge is all built up...
4. London Bridge is falling down...
5. Take the key and lock him/her up...
6. Off to prison you must go...

Motions

Two children stand and face each other. Before each round of the game, these two children secretly decide which one will be "pins" and which one will be "needles." The rest of the group walks in a figure-eight pattern around the two children. The group continues walking during the second verse when the pair makes an arch with one hand and during the third verse when they make an arch with two hands. On the last line of the fourth verse, one child is caught by the two forming the arch. During the fifth verse, the two forming the arch gently push and pull the child caught in the middle. During the sixth verse, the "captured" one chooses "pins" or "needles" and stands behind the corresponding child. After the last child chooses "pins" or "needles," everyone grabs the waist of the person in front, and a tug of war ensues.

The Needle's Eye (Version 1)

Oh, the nee-dle's eye that doth sup-ply the thread that runs so

tru-ly, There is man-y a lass that I let pass, Be-cause I want-ed
There is man-y a beau that I let go, Be-cause I want-ed

you.— Be-cause I want-ed you, Be-cause I want-ed
you.—

you, There's man-y a lass that I let pass, be-cause I want-ed
beau go

you. You, you, you.— Be-cause I want-ed you.

Motions

Two children stand and hold hands to form an arch. One child represents "pins" and one represents "needles." The other children pass under the arch while walking in a circle. On the last line one child is caught by the arch and must choose between "pins" or "needles." She or he then stands behind the corresponding child. After the last child chooses "pins" or "needles," there is a tug of war between the two sides with each child holding onto the waist of the child in front of him or her.

The Needle's Eye (Version 2)

The nee-dle's eye no one can pass, The thread that's drawn so true:— It has caught man-y a love-ly lass, And now it has caught you.— You— look so neat,— And you look so sweet,— We do in-tend, Be-fore we end, To see this cou-ple meet.

Motions

One boy (the "gent") and one girl (the "lady") hold hands and make an arch. The others form a circle and pass under the arch. On the words "caught you," the couple lowers the arch and "captures" the person that is passing under. At the end of the song, the "captured" person changes places with the lady (if a girl) or with the gent (if a boy). The game repeats.

Oranges and Lemons

"Or-anges and lem-ons" say the bells of St. Clem-ent's. "You

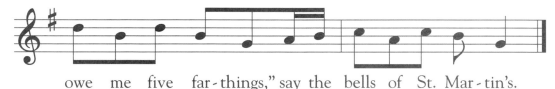

owe me five far-things," say the bells of St. Mar-tin's.

Additional Verses

"When will you pay me?" say the
bells of Old Bailey.

"When I grow rich," say the bells of
Shoreditch.

"Pray, when will that be?" say the
bells of Stephney.

"I'm sure I don't know," says the great
bell at Bow.

"Bull's eyes and targets," say the bells
of St. Marg'ret's.

"Brickbats and tiles," say the bells of
St. Giles.

"Pancakes and fritters," say the bells
of St. Peter's.

"Two sticks and an apple," say the
bells at Whitechapel.

"Old Father Baldpate," say the slow
bells at Aldgate.

"Maids in white aprons," say the bells
at St. Catherine's.

"Pokers and tongs," say the bells at
St. John's.

"Kettles and pans," say the bells at
St. Anne's.

*Only the first verse is sung when playing
the game.*

Motions

*Two children hold hands and lift them to
form an arch. One child will be "oranges"
and the other will be "lemons." The rest of
the children form a circle and pass under
the arch. At the end of the song,
the arch drops and "captures" one of the
children. The "captured" child whispers
"oranges" or "lemons" into the ear of one
of the children forming the arch and stands
behind the corresponding child. When all
the children have passed under the arch
and are standing in one of the lines,
everyone grabs the waist of the person in
front, and a tug of war ensues.*

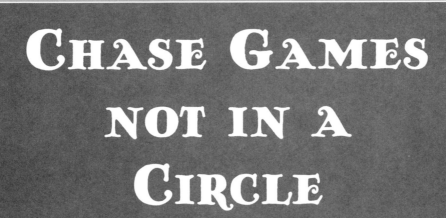

CHASE GAMES NOT IN A CIRCLE

Blackhorn

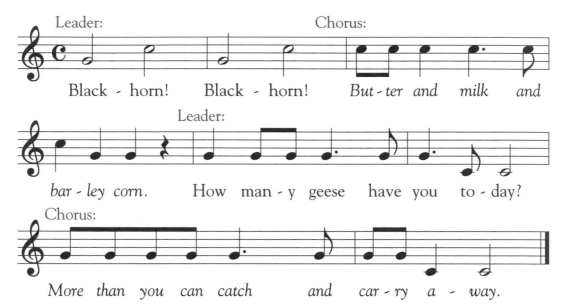

Leader: Black - horn! Black - horn! **Chorus:** But - ter and milk and bar - ley corn.

Leader: How man - y geese have you to - day?

Chorus: More than you can catch and car - ry a - way.

Motions

The group stands at one end of the room or playing field. One person (the hunter) stands in the middle of the room. The call and response is sung. At the end of the song, everyone runs to the other end of the room. The hunter tries to tag as many children as possible. Those who are tagged stay in the center and help tag the others when the song repeats. Continue the game until everyone has been tagged. The last person tagged becomes the new hunter.

Chickama, Chickama

Chick - a - ma, Chick - a - ma, Cra - ney, crow,

Went to the well to wash his toe.

When he got there his chick - en was gone. "What

time is it, old witch?" "One!"

Motions

One person (the witch) stands in the center of the room. All the others stand at one end of the room and sing the song. At the end of the song, the witch shouts "one," and everyone tries to run to the other end of the room without being caught. All those who are "tagged" stay in the center and help tag others when the game repeats. The last one caught becomes the next witch.

How Many Miles to London Town?

How man-y miles to Lon-don town? Four score and ten!

Can I get there by can-dle-light? Yes! and back a-gain!

Motions

The group stands at one end of the room with one person in the middle. At the end of the song, everyone runs to the other end of the room while the one in the middle tries to tag other children. Those "tagged" stay in the center and try to catch others on the next crossing. The last one tagged becomes the new one in the center and the game begins again.

Old Raggy

Old Rag-gy, Old Rag-gy, with your pack on your back.

Old Rag-gy, Old Rag-gy, put down your load.

Can it be can-dy bars, toy trains or lit-tle cars?

O-pen it, o-pen it. Don't let us see.

Motions

The group stands at one end of the room with one person ("Old Raggy") in the middle. The group sings the song. "Old Raggy" pretends to pull various "gifts" from an imaginary bag. The group responds to desirable gifts with a "Mmmmmm" sound. The group responds to undesirable gifts with an "Ewwwwww" sound. When "Old Raggy" pretends to pull "dogs to bite you" out of the bag, all of the children run from one end of the room to the other while "Old Raggy" tries to tag as many as possible. Those who have been tagged stay in the center and help "Old Raggy" tag others after each repetition until only one child is left. That child becomes the new "Old Raggy" and the game begins again.

Index